ALL ABOUT SUMMER

WEATHER

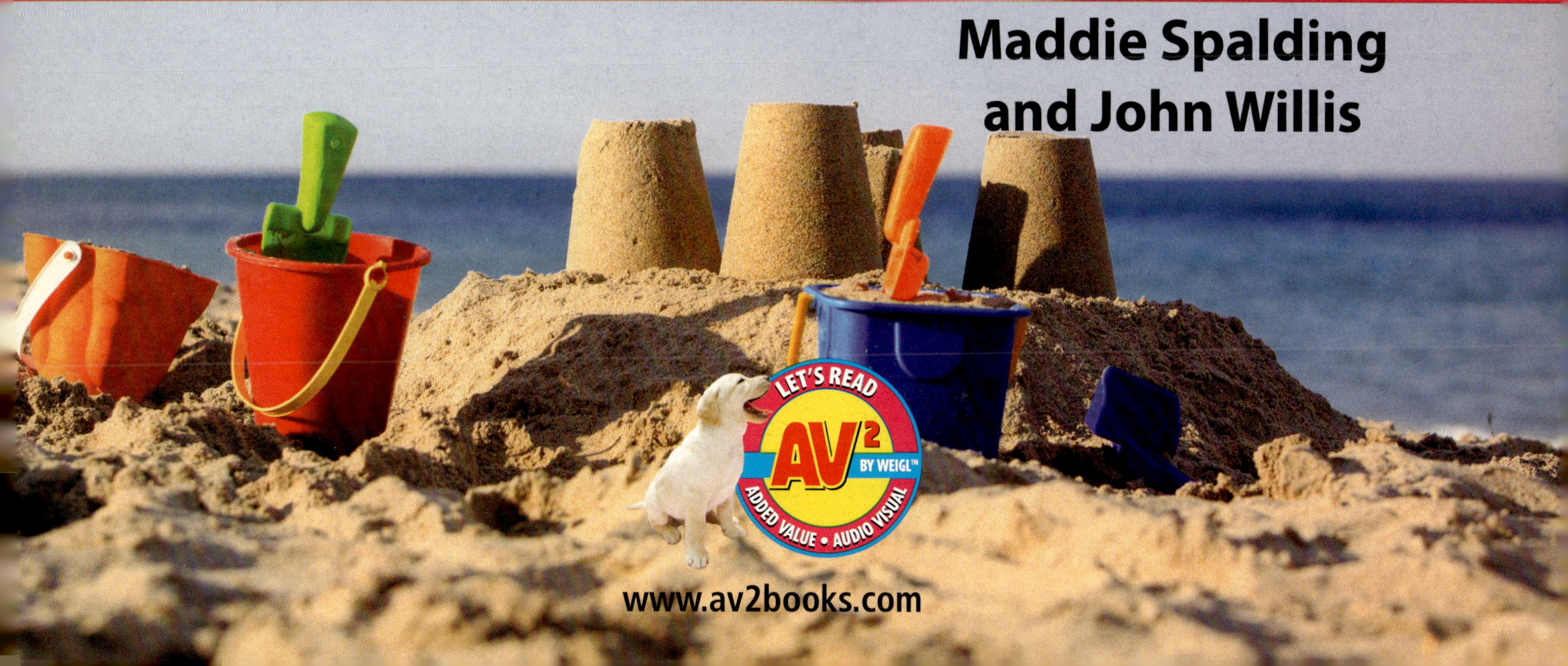

Maddie Spalding
and John Willis

LET'S READ AV² BY WEIGL™ ADDED VALUE • AUDIO VISUAL

www.av2books.com

Go to www.av2books.com, and enter this book's unique code.

BOOK CODE

AVL72272

AV^2 by Weigl brings you media enhanced books that support active learning.

AV^2 provides enriched content that supplements and complements this book. Weigl's AV^2 books strive to create inspired learning and engage young minds in a total learning experience.

Your AV^2 Media Enhanced books come alive with...

Audio
Listen to sections of the book read aloud.

Video
Watch informative video clips.

Embedded Weblinks
Gain additional information for research.

Try This!
Complete activities and hands-on experiments.

Key Words
Study vocabulary, and complete a matching word activity.

Quizzes
Test your knowledge.

Slide Show
View images and captions, and prepare a presentation.

... and much, much more!

Published by AV^2 by Weigl
350 5th Avenue, 59th Floor New York, NY 10118
Website: www.av2books.com

Library of Congress Cataloging-in-Publication Data

Names: Spalding, Maddie, 1990- author. | Willis, John, 1989- author.
Title: Weather / Maddie Spalding and John Willis.
Description: New York : AV^2 by Weigl, [2019] | Series: All about summer |
Audience: K to grade 3. | Includes index.
Identifiers: LCCN 2018053403 (print) | LCCN 2018055213 (ebook) |
ISBN 9781489696878 (Multi User ebook) | ISBN 9781489696885 (Single User ebook) |
ISBN 9781489696854 (hardcover : alk. paper) | ISBN 9781489696861 (softcover : alk. paper)
Subjects: LCSH: Weather--Juvenile literature. | Meteorology--Juvenile literature.
Classification: LCC QC981.3 (ebook) | LCC QC981.3 .S655 2019 (print) | DDC 551.5--dc23
LC record available at https://lccn.loc.gov/2018053403

Printed in the United States of America in Brainerd, Minnesota
1 2 3 4 5 6 7 8 9 0 22 21 20 19 18

122018
102918

Project Coordinator: John Willis Designer: Ana María Vidal

Every reasonable effort has been made to trace ownership and to obtain permission to reprint copyright material.
The publishers would be pleased to have any errors or omissions brought to their attention so that they may be corrected in subsequent printings.
Weigl acknowledges Getty Images and iStock as the primary image suppliers for this title.

First published by The Child's World in 2018

WEATHER

In this book, you will learn about

what it is

what it does

how it changes

and much more!

Summer Heat

The Sun shines.
It is a hot summer day.

The city of Yuma, Arizona, gets more sunlight than any other place on Earth.

Earth tilts. This makes the seasons. Part of Earth tilts toward the Sun in summer.

There is more sunlight
in summer.
The weather gets hotter.

California's **Death Valley** had the **hottest temperature** ever recorded in the United States.

There are storms in summer.
Clouds form in the sky.
It starts to rain.

The rain makes puddles.
Rain helps plants grow.

We see lightning.
We hear thunder.

Lightning strikes Earth about **8 million** times **each day**.

We wear shorts
in summer.
We also wear T-shirts.

We drink cold water.
This keeps us cool.

Fall comes after summer.
The weather gets colder.

In the United States, the **last day** of summer is on **September 21** or **22**.

Rain Cloud Craft

Make your own rain cloud!

Supplies:

- blue construction paper
- blue streamers
- pencil
- scissors
- glue
- cotton balls

Instructions:

1. Draw a cloud shape on the blue paper. Cut out the cloud with the scissors.
2. Dab glue onto the cloud. Glue cotton balls on so that they cover the entire cloud.
3. Cut the streamers into strips. Glue the streamers onto the back of the cloud. The streamers will look like rain.

KEY WORDS

Research has shown that as much as 65 percent of all written material published in English is made up of 300 words. These 300 words cannot be taught using pictures or learned by sounding them out. They must be recognized by sight. This book contains 42 common sight words to help young readers improve their reading fluency and comprehension. This book also teaches young readers several important content words, such as proper nouns. These words are paired with pictures to aid in learning and improve understanding.

Page	Sight Words First Appearance
4	a, day, is, it, the
5	any, city, Earth, gets, more, of, on, other, place, than
7	in, makes, part, this
8	there
9	had, states
11	are, starts, to
12	grow, helps, plants
14	hear, see, we
15	about, each, times
16	also
19	keeps, us, water
20	after, comes
21	last, or

Page	Content Words First Appearance
4	summer, Sun
5	Arizona, sunlight, Yuma
7	seasons
8	weather
9	California, Death Valley, temperature
11	clouds, rain, sky, storms
12	puddles
14	lightning, thunder
16	shorts, T-shirts
20	fall
21	September

Check out www.av2books.com for activities, videos, audio clips, and more!

1. **Go to www.av2books.com.**
2. **Enter book code.** AVL72272
3. **Fuel your imagination online!**

www.av2books.com